WEB WISDOM

Make the Most of Facebook and Other Social Media

Cathleen Small

Cavendish
Square
New York

For Theo, who I'm certain will someday parlay his love of elevators and rock music into some strange (and hopefully profitable) career. If anyone can do it, you can!

Published in 2015 by Cavendish Square Publishing, LLC
243 5th Avenue, Suite 136, New York, NY 10016

First Edition

Website: cavendishsq.com

CPSIA Compliance Information: Batch #WW15CSQ

All websites were available and accurate when this book was sent to press.

Library of Congress Cataloging-in-Publication Data

Small, Cathleen.
Make the most of Facebook and other social media / Cathleen Small.
pages cm. — (Web wisdom)
Includes bibliographical references and index.
ISBN 978-1-50260-197-1 (hardcover) ISBN 978-1-50260-196-4 (ebook)
1. Online social networks—Juvenile literature. 2. Social media—Juvenile literature. I. Title.

HM742.S622 2015
302.23'1—dc23

2014021296

Editor: Andrew Coddington
Senior Copy Editor: Wendy A. Reynolds
Art Director: Jeffrey Talbot
Designer: Douglas Brooks
Senior Production Manager: Jennifer Ryder-Talbot
Production Editor: David McNamara
Photo Research by J8 Media

The photopraphs in this book are used permission and through the courtsety of: Cover photo by Bloom Design/Shutterstock.com; Jamie Grill/The Image Bank/Getty Images, 4; Justin Sullivan/Getty Images News, 7; Laki9851/iStock Editorial/Thinkstock, 8; Blend Images – John Lund/Brand X Images/Getty Images, 10; Westend61 / Westend61, 11; Madredus/iStock/Thinkstock, 11; Peathegee Inc/Blend Images/Getty Images, 12; milos-kreckovic/© iStockphoto.com, 14; JGI/Jamie Grill/Blend Images/Getty Images, 16; Hill Street Studios/Blend Images/Getty Images, 20; nensuria/iStock/Thinkstock, 22; Dimitri Otis/Stone/Getty Images, 24; Doug Brooks for Cavendish Square, 25; Tim Robberts/Taxi/Getty Images, 26; Doug Brooks for Cavendish Square, 28; Alex Bramwell/Moment/Getty Images, 29; Courtesy Facebook and Cathleen Small, 30; Ryan McVay/Stone/Getty Images, 32; Echo/Cultura/Getty Images, 34; Bill Reitzel/Digital Vision/Getty Images, 35; VICTOR HABBICK VISIONS/Science Photo Library/Getty Images, 38; Jim Spellman/WireImage/Getty Images, 41.

Printed in the United States of America

Contents

CHAPTER 1

What Is Social Media?

You've likely heard the term **social media**, and you may even have a broad idea of what it is. Sites such as Facebook, Twitter, and Vine probably jump to mind, and you can probably name a few more.

These are good examples, but to really understand what social media is and how it can work for you, we should start with a definition. Simply put, social media is made up of virtual **communities** where people interact and share information. That information can be words, pictures, videos, or even audio clips. A **social network** is a place to share your ideas, in whatever form, and to interact with others' ideas, too.

How It Began

Social media exists on the Internet—so without the Internet, there is no social media. Although the idea of the Internet first came into being in the early 1960s, the Internet as we know it wasn't created until around the early 1990s, and it wasn't until the later 1990s and early 2000s that many people had access to the Internet from their homes.

When personal Internet use first became more widespread, most people used it to email, look things up, and sometimes visit **chat rooms**. Chat rooms were the earliest social networks, since people would gather there to, well, chat. However, people didn't have permanent, established accounts with chat rooms. They would just pop in from time to time and chat with whomever else was in the "room."

The Social Networks

Friendster, launched in 2002, is believed to be the first true social network in the U.S. MySpace followed soon after, in 2003, and many people consider that to be the first major social network in the U.S. MySpace allowed users to create pages featuring their interests, post videos and pictures, and more. At its peak, MySpace had 75 million users. That number has since declined, and today it's mostly used by musicians and bands sharing their music.

Facebook was created in 2004 by Mark Zuckerberg, a student at Harvard who created the network for college students. In 2006, Facebook became available to the general public, and anyone over the age of thirteen could open a Facebook account.

Many people also consider YouTube to be a social network because users can post videos and other users can view and comment on them. YouTube began in 2005 and is still very popular in the social networking world. In fact, YouTube boasts more than four billion video views every day.

By 2006, when Twitter burst onto the scene, MySpace was still the most popular social networking site, although within two years Facebook would take over as the most popular. Nowadays, Facebook has more than 1.2 billion users, compared to MySpace's 36 million. Twitter has more than 200 million active users. The relatively

Mark Zuckerberg created Facebook in 2004, while he was a student at Harvard University.

new social media **platform** Instagram, which was launched in 2010, has 150 million users.

The New Generation of Social Media Sites

Social media evolves so rapidly that it's hard to nail down what's popular on any given day. For example, MySpace was once the king of social media sites, but it was quickly dethroned by Facebook. Still, some social networks have staying power, and Facebook is probably the biggest one.

In 2014, Facebook had 1.28 billion total users and 680 million Facebook Mobile users. Forty-eight percent of Facebook users log on to the network at least once a day, and the average

Most social media sites offer mobile versions for smartphones, such as Facebook Mobile.

amount of time spent on Facebook is eighteen minutes per visit. Although some say that Facebook is no longer the biggest player in the social networking world, statistics say otherwise. In fact, the number of Facebook users increased by 22 percent from 2012 to 2013. Among teenagers, Facebook is still the most popular social network, with 77 percent of online teens using it.

Other social media sites popular among teens include Twitter and Instagram. Vine and Snapchat are also gaining in popularity. According to a 2014 Pew Research study of teens with social media accounts, 94 percent had Facebook accounts, 26 percent had Twitter accounts, and 11 percent had Instagram accounts. The study did not cover Vine or Snapchat, but recent reports suggest that Vine has about thirteen million users, and Snapchat has about twenty-six million.

Which Social Network Is Right for You?

The statistics for social media are enough to make your head spin. The number of options are almost as mind-boggling, given the number of new social networks that have been cropping up. How do you decide which one is right for you?

You don't have to choose just one! Try out as many as you want, and see which you like.

Find out which social networks your friends are using most, and you'll probably find you naturally gravitate toward those networks.

The other cool thing about social networks is that many "play nicely" together and allow you to **cross-post**. You can tweet on Twitter and have it post to your Facebook account, your Tumblr blog, and more. The same is true with Instagram. Facebook "like" and "post" buttons are virtually everywhere across the Internet, allowing you to quickly announce things like your latest YouTube video.

Like sharing pictures? Try Instagram!

AGE REQUIREMENTS

A recent study from Knowthenet, a British company whose goal is to make the Internet a safer, more secure place, found that 59 percent of kids join social networks before they turn ten. This is interesting because there are minimum age requirements on most social media sites. You must be thirteen years old to sign up for a Facebook or Instagram account, for example. For those sites that don't post a definite minimum age, such as Twitter, the Children's Online Privacy Protection Act of 1998 states that children in the United States must be at least thirteen years old to use most social media sites.

However, many social networks consider **parental consent** to be a reasonable compromise. If you're under thirteen years old and your parent or guardian sets up an account for you, they are okay with that. They simply warn you and your parent(s) to be aware that some content may be inappropriate.

CHAPTER 2

Why Use Social Media?

Now that you have a better idea of what exactly social media is and where it came from, let's talk about why you might want to use it. While "because everyone is doing it" isn't a good motive to do much of anything, there are definitely many reasons why everyone is using social media.

Staying in Touch

Years ago, people made friends in their neighborhood and at school, and those people became an individual's core social group. Friends who lived far away were few and far between, and it took some effort to keep in touch with them.

Since the invention of the Internet and social media sites, keeping in touch with friends and family is easier than ever, even those who live far away. In a matter of seconds, you can dash off a message to a friend halfway across the globe. On Facebook, you can write a quick post on a friend's **Timeline**, or send your friend a private message. You can write a general post that will show up on all of your Facebook friends' News Feeds. Plus, if you want to be sure a particular person sees a post, you can "tag" that person in the post.

Social networks also let you keep in touch visually. Post as many pictures as you want, whenever you want, and all your friends can see them. You can also adjust your privacy settings so only certain people can see them.

Many platforms also allow you to post videos. What if Grandma can't come to your piano recital,

Recording a video and posting it to social media is a great way to share the moment with friends.

but really wants to see you play? Have someone in the audience take a video with a smartphone or video camera, and you can easily upload it to social media for all your friends and family to enjoy.

Connecting with New Friends

Social media isn't just for keeping in touch with old friends and faraway family members, though. It's also for making new friends. With social media, your potential friend pool is enormous. You can join groups to find friends with common interests, but that's not the only way to make new friends on social media. You can also find new friends through your existing friends.

BE SAFE!

Making new friends on social media is great, whether they are friends-of-friends or people you meet in a group. However, please, please be careful. **Online predators** are a very real threat, and one you need to be aware of. No matter how friendly someone seems on social media, keep your personal information, such as your address, phone number, name of your school or workplace, and so on, private. If anyone suggests that you meet in person, do not do so without first talking to your parent or guardian. The person may indeed be a great, legitimate new friend, but remember that online predators are very, very skilled at pretending to be something they're not.

Suppose a friend from school is having a big party to celebrate her birthday. When you arrive, you'll probably know several people there from school. There may also be other people you haven't met before. Perhaps the birthday girl has also invited her friends from church or from some other after-school or weekend activity. Suddenly, you're introduced to some new potential friends.

Social media works the same way. When your friends post something on social media, their friends may comment on it, and you may find that you have something in common with some of those people. Say your friend posts a picture from a horseback-riding competition she participated

You might be surprised by how many new friends you can meet through social media.

in on her Facebook page, and you comment on the picture because you enjoy horseback riding, too. Chances are, many of the other people who comment on that picture are also horse fans. Over time, you may see the same people commenting on your friend's posts, and you may reach out to those people and become Facebook friends with them. Those friendships may start on social media, but they can easily bloom into something more. This is not Facebook-specific, by the way. The same connections can happen on any social media site.

If you're wondering how one even goes about finding people with a common interest, one answer is **hashtags**. People on social media often use hashtags to identify their posts, and those hashtags can enable others to search for common topics. Another way you might find people with common interests is simply luck. Thinking back to the example of your friend who posted the picture about her horseback-riding competition, you both commented on your mutual friend's post, and now you've met and realized you have something in common!

Collaborating with Others

Keeping in touch with old friends and making new ones are both prime uses for social media. If that's not enough reason to make you want to join a social media platform (or three!), think about another aspect: **collaboration**.

With social media, you have a huge pool of collaborators at your fingertips. Need a quick answer to something? Tweet your question, or post it on Facebook. Want an opinion on a new hairstyle you're thinking of trying? Post a picture on Instagram or Facebook and ask for feedback. Want someone to look over an essay you're working hard on? Ask your friends on social media if anyone is willing to take a quick look for you. Chances are, someone will say yes.

You can also collaborate to promote a cause on social media. Suppose you're fundraising for a 5k charity run. You can post the details about your endeavor to social media and ask people if they're interested in joining you or contributing. The possibilities really are endless.

The Types of Social Media Sites

Now that you know what you can do on social media, let's talk a bit about the kinds of social media sites that exist. There is a lot of overlap in what social media platforms allow you to do, but you can roughly divide them into two categories, which are text-focused sites and **multimedia**-focused sites.

Text-Focused Sites

Make no mistake: most text-focused social media sites do allow you to post pictures and other media, but they also support text posts. These are sites such as Facebook and Twitter.

Twitter famously began as a site where you could send out short, 140-character "tweets" about whatever was on your mind. While its platform now allows users to tweet images and Vine videos, Twitter is still best known as a text-based social media site.

Facebook, too, is largely text-focused. It allows you to post photos and videos, and many people do, but most people use it to share their thoughts in writing. Unlike Twitter, Facebook doesn't give you a character limit, so you can type as much as you want in a text post.

Multimedia-Focused Sites

Currently, two of the most popular multimedia-focused social media sites are Instagram and Vine. Instagram was created for posting pictures, though you can now record short videos. Vine allows you to post short, looping video clips. Although Instagram allows you to caption your photos and Vine lets you caption your videos, both of these are primarily image-based services.

Snapchat, too, is a multimedia-focused site. Like Instagram and Vine, Snapchat allows you to caption photos and video clips, so there is a text element to it. However, the photo or video is the main focus of the application.

How does Snapchat differ from Instagram and Vine? Instagram and Vine posts are permanent unless you purposely delete them, but Snapchat posts will always automatically disappear after ten seconds of viewing. The creators of Snapchat wanted to create a place where people could be totally honest and open, without worrying that their funny image or ranting caption would be on the Internet forever. With Snapchat, it's there and then it's gone.

Remember that on most social media sites, what you post is there to stay, and future college admissions reps and employers may search through social media to find out more about you. Be sure what you post is something you don't mind them finding!

SOCIAL MEDIA AND YOUR FUTURE COLLEGE OR EMPLOYMENT PROSPECTS

What you post on the Internet is very, very hard to fully "erase." On most social networks, once you post something, it's out there. You can delete the post, but if people have already seen it, it may be impossible to fully remove its existence. This can come back to haunt you later. More and more colleges and potential employers are researching the social media posts of prospective students or employees as part of their screening process. If you have a bunch of inappropriate or insensitive pictures or posts floating around, it's not going to look particularly promising to the college you're hoping to attend, or the employer you're hoping to impress.

In fact, a recent survey by Kaplan Test Prep showed that approximately one of every three colleges you apply to is going to look at your social media profile or page and potentially make a judgment about your candidacy based partly on what they see. This can be a good thing for you if your social media usage is largely positive. It can negatively affect your chances if you use social media as a place to display your rowdy antics or to air your complaints about others.

Saying angry things about coworkers or classmates is never a good idea, either. The chances of your rant getting back to that person (or someone related to him or her) are pretty strong. If whatever you said isn't something you would say to that person's face, you probably don't want to post it.

So think, "Is this really something I want out there forever?" before you click the "post" button.

CHAPTER 3

Advanced Features of Social Media

You can use social media as part of your everyday life to keep in touch with friends and family and to make new friends. It's as simple as posting a picture, a video, or your thoughts in text form. Or, you can even just comment on posts by others if you don't feel inspired to create your own posts. If you find you enjoy being part of a social network, there's a lot more you can do with social media.

Cross-Platform Posting

The whole point of posting on social media is to reach your audience, right? You want people to know what you're thinking or see what you're doing. It's fun to share that picture of you making the game-winning touchdown or of you spending a lazy afternoon at the pool with friends. Social media also immediately gives you a wide audience—all of your friends on that particular social media platform will see your post. However, what if your friends are spread across multiple platforms? What if some use Instagram, others prefer Facebook, and still others simply follow your tweets? Cross-platform posting may be the answer you're looking for.

The great thing about social media is that the various platforms generally make it very easy for you to send your posts to multiple platforms in real time. On Twitter, for example, you can configure your profile so that all of your tweets are immediately posted on your Facebook Timeline, too. Vine allows you to share your video to Facebook or Twitter, or you can copy and embed **code** to share it on a website. Instagram allows you to instantly share to

Your network on social media can quickly become a vast web!

FACEBOOK PAGES VERSUS GROUPS

In the early days of Facebook, groups were quite popular. More recently, pages have become more popular. For example, if you're a fan of a particular musical artist, it's likely that artist has a page. You can "like" the page, and you'll immediately receive updates from the page in your News Feed. You can also connect with other fans that way.

Why do groups still exist? The biggest answer is privacy. Facebook pages are always public, whereas groups can be set to private or even secret, so that people not in the group won't be able to access it or see members' posts.

Social media is a very public place, and there are some things about your life you might like to keep private. My group of mothers of children with Down syndrome is set to private, for example, and it's not because any of us hides the fact that our children share this chromosomal abnormality. Rather, it's because we talk about topics that are sometimes rather private and personal in nature, and we all feel more comfortable sharing our honest, true feelings knowing that the group is private and only those in it can see the posts.

You may be very open about most things in your life, but if you want some privacy about a particular topic, groups are a good place to find it.

Facebook, Twitter, Tumblr, and Flickr. You can even link your Facebook profile to Twitter so that your Twitter followers see your Facebook updates. In short, the social networks make it easy to keep all of your friends and followers in the loop with just a few quick button-clicks.

Joining Groups

You have already learned about using social media to find new friends, as well as keep in touch with your existing friends and family. One way you can find new friends on social media is by joining groups. This allows you to find people with similar interests.

There are groups for everything on Facebook. Many communities have groups. You can easily join one to meet other people who live in your area.

Can't find a Facebook group that fits your interests? Why not create a group yourself? You're sure to find others with shared interests.

Other groups are made up of people around the world who share similar interests. Maybe you're an aspiring musician who enjoys a particular style of music. Search for a group devoted to that type of music, and you're likely to find one (if not more!). If you don't find a group that fits your particular interests, you can always create one of your own.

Using Hashtags

Suppose you want to start a group. How do you find people with similar interests to join it? You may already know some, just by virtue of connections you've made on social media. Hashtags are another way to do it.

Simply put, hashtags are a way to identify messages or posts about a certain topic. A hashtag is a word or phrase without spaces preceded by the pound symbol (#). When users search for or click on a hashtag on social media, the site immediately finds posts with similar hashtags. For example, I can find loads of posts about Down syndrome by entering #downsyndrome. Another example is the popular feature on Instagram and Facebook called "Throwback Thursday," where people post old pictures of themselves and add the hashtag #tbt (short for "Throwback Thursday") to the comment. If you type #tbt into a social media search, you will quickly find a ton of throwback photos.

Hashtags originated for public use on Twitter. The first hashtag on social media was #barcamp, created by Chris Messina, who thought it would be a good way to organize communications on a particular topic. (Barcamp was a series of global-technology gatherings organized by Messina.) The trend caught on, and now hashtags are used on a lot of social media. The funny thing is, the founder of Twitter didn't like hashtags and thought them "too nerdy" to ever go mainstream—proof that even founders of major companies can be wrong!

Hashtags are so popular now that some people use them just as a joke, or to convey an emotion. During finals week at school, you might add a hashtag to a post saying something like #ineedavacation. They're a short, quick way to express what you're feeling. In their true use,

Your parents knew this symbol as the pound or number sign. Nowadays, it's more widely recognized as the symbol for a hashtag.

You can make a bold statement with a simple hashtag.

however, hashtags are a helpful way to link your posts to others on a similar subject. Let's say you are competing in a regional show choir competition. Maybe you tag your posts with #showchoir2014. Then anyone else posting on that same topic could use the same hashtag so that your posts would be somewhat linked in the social media world. You could even use hashtags to identify your posts on a specific cause.

Promoting a Cause

Perhaps you're raising money for a charity, or maybe you just want to bring awareness to a topic. Social media is a great way to promote a cause.

For example, as I mentioned earlier, one of my sons has Down syndrome. That subject is near and dear to my heart, so I use social networks to bring awareness about Down syndrome to my friends,

The #tbt (Throwback Thursday) feature has become a fun addition to Facebook and Instagram.

family, and followers on social media. October is Down Syndrome Awareness Month, so last October I featured a different child with Down syndrome every day on my Facebook page, with a beautiful picture and some information about that specific child in each post. I used the hashtag #downsyndromeawareness to classify all of those posts as related to Down Syndrome Awareness Month. I also enabled my privacy settings to allow my friends to share those posts on their Timelines, which many did. By the end of the month, we had opened a lot of eyes about the beautiful children born with this condition. In addition, I raised $1,500 for our local Down syndrome association by using social media to post about our annual October fundraising walk.

So what interests you? What topic is near and dear to your heart? What do you want people to know more about? If there's something weighing on your mind or your heart, think of how you can use social media to share your knowledge about the subject and bring awareness to others.

Suppose you're an animal lover, and on the weekends you volunteer with a local animal rescue organization. Such organizations typically need two things: people to provide homes for the rescue animals, and people to provide money to cover the care for the animals. If you want to help the organization, you can easily do so with social media. Did the organization just take in a litter of puppies that need homes? You could tweet pictures of them and cross-post to your Facebook and other social media accounts with information about how people can adopt one if they're interested. Want to help raise money for the organization? There are online tools you can use to set up fundraisers (GoFundMe. com is a big one), create fundraising goals, and promote your cause on social media.

As with almost anything in the online world, the possibilities are endless. Think about how you can use social media to share what's important to you. I guarantee you will find more ways than you can even imagine.

CHAPTER 4

Social Networks in Action

By now you've learned a lot about social media. You know how it all started, and you know about some of the most popular sites. You also know what the biggest current platforms in the social media world are, and that this coveted spot is likely to change at any time. Plus, you learned how you can use social media most effectively to keep in touch with people, find new friends, and even promote causes. Now let's take a look at how some young people have used social media to make a difference in their lives, and in the lives of others.

Using Social Media to Meet People

Twelve-year-old Theo has moved to a new city, where he pretty much doesn't know anyone. He wants to keep in touch with his friends from his old school and neighborhood, but he also wants to meet new people.

Keeping in touch with his old friends is pretty easy, because many of them have Facebook accounts. Those who don't use Instagram and Snapchat. He quickly sets up accounts on those platforms and connects with all his old friends.

Making new friends is more challenging, so he has to think outside the box. Theo has two great loves in life: elevators and rock music. He decides to go about finding some new friends by looking for people with similar interests.

Elevators are a pretty specific interest, and most elevator fans happen to be adults. So, Theo joins a couple of Facebook groups for people who love

Use social media to make new friends and keep in touch with old ones.

elevators and subscribes to the YouTube channels of his favorite elevator videographers (yes, they exist!), but he realizes that these friends will be online-only, given that most don't live in the area, and his parents have pretty strict rules about him not meeting people he's met on social media in person. (Remember, safety first!)

How does he find some local friends? With a little bit of detective work, Theo discovers that his new school has a Facebook group set up, so he joins the group. When he does, he recognizes the names of a few of his classmates and sends them friend requests. They quickly add him to their Friends Lists,

Let your Facebook Friends List know about upcoming events—like your band's gig!

and voila! The beginnings of multiple friendships are born.

Through a little more detective work, Theo discovers a few groups that interest him in his new city—one of which is a rock band for kids, run by a local music teacher. He talks to his parents, who agree to let him try out the class and join the band. Theo is very excited about the opportunity to learn to play electric guitar with a band, and it's an opportunity he never would've found if he hadn't been searching local groups on social media. The band posts performance videos on YouTube and clips of videos on Vine and Instagram, which lead to more friend connections for Theo. He may not go on to become a world-famous guitarist, but if nothing else, he has enjoyed learning to play with the band, and he makes some great lifelong friends.

Finding Fame on Social Media

Most people use social media simply to connect with other people. In some cases, however, people find fame on social media. It's not terribly common, but it's not unheard of.

Take the case of Nash Grier, a sixteen-year-old from North Carolina who has found fame on Vine. As of this writing, he is currently the top Vine user in the world, with more than 7.8 million followers globally. How did he get so famous? People enjoy his Vines, which mix humor, angst, song parodies, and slapstick.

Nash says that the most important component to his Vines is originality. He protects his work using the free, easy-to-use copyright licenses on the Creative Commons website, CreativeCommons.org. Doing this ensures that Nash receives credit whenever someone reposts or uses part of one of his Vines.

Is there a bonus to being famous on social media? Well, sometimes it can lead to job opportunities. Several international businesses are considering Nash for branding opportunities, and people have contacted him to license his Vines, both of which would lead to income for him. However, the biggest incentive for Nash is the one that led him to creating Vines in the first place—he just likes to make people laugh.

YouTube is another social media platform where people have found fame. One such story involves eighteen-year-old Bethany Mota, who has been posting videos since 2009 and today has more than 5.9 million subscribers to her channel— five times more than Taylor Swift has. Bethany reviews makeup, clothes, and mall finds, but she also posts messages about self-confidence and empowerment. Bethany's YouTube fame nets her an

RESPONSIBLE POSTING AND CYBERBULLYING

Cyberbullying, or using the Internet to harass another person, has been getting a lot of attention recently. Social media is a wonderful thing in that it can bring people together. However, the downside to social media is that the relative anonymity of the Internet can make people feel they can say whatever they want. You will find that people can be incredibly cruel on social media. You'll need to have a thick skin to shrug off some of the comments you see.

As someone involved in the disability **community**, I have personally seen the negative side of social media, where incredible $40,000 per month in income, and she has recently signed a design deal with the clothing company Aéropostale.

Remember, though, that along with fame can come criticism. When Bethany was thirteen years old, someone created a MySpace page in her name and used it to post "vicious" stories about her. Bethany was so upset that she stayed in her room all day, watching videos of girls trying on clothes or experimenting with hairstyles, instead of interacting with people.

people make thoughtless, cruel comments. As someone new to social media, you need to develop self-confidence and keep in mind that what people say about you on these sites doesn't really reflect you. You must also make sure that you are a responsible poster who doesn't engage in that sort of thoughtless behavior. "If you can't say anything nice, don't say anything at all" holds doubly true on social media.

The penalties for cyberbullying are getting stiffer. Think before you post. You don't want to find yourself getting punished for cyberbullying just because you made what you thought was a relatively innocent, funny comment on social media. Always keep in mind that words can hurt, and if they're delivered anonymously in an online forum instead of in person, they can hurt all the more.

Bethany's story has a happy ending: watching those videos encouraged Bethany to try her hand at making her own, and she became very successful at it. For some people, however, that sort of negative criticism can be devastating, and the results can be tragic. Just remember not to take Internet criticism and cyberbullying to heart. If it does happen and you're feeling bad about it, talk to someone. Don't simply close yourself up like Bethany did. Find a parent or a trusted adult, and have them help you work through the negative feelings that can come about from something like this. Always remember that the point of using social media is to have fun and connect with people. Don't let a few cyberbullies spoil the experience for you!

Keep in mind that while your friends on Facebook, Twitter, Instagram, and other social media platforms are fun to spend time with online, you should also build your own "social network" in the real world as well. Spend time outdoors, get together with family members and classmates, or join an after-school program or sports team. Remember, balance between the real world and the cyber world is the key to being truly social!

Bethany Mota has used social media to create an incredibly lucrative business for herself.

GLOSSARY

chat room A place on the Internet where users can communicate. Chat rooms typically focus on a particular topic.

code The "language" used by a computer or an application. Code is a collection of instructions that tell a program to do something.

collaboration The act of working with others to solve a problem or to create something.

community A group of people who generally have something in common. People who use social media are often part of numerous different online communities.

cross-post Posting the same text, picture, video, or audio clip simultaneously on multiple social media platforms.

cyberbullying Bullying that is done using electronic technology, including text messages, chats, websites, and social media.

hashtag A word or phrase that is preceded by a number sign, or hash mark (#). Hashtags are used to classify topics on social media.

multimedia Different types of artistic or communicative media, such as pictures, videos, audio clips, and so on.

online predator A person who uses the Internet to commit crimes. Although online predators don't necessarily have to be sexual predators, many are.

parental consent Your parent's or legal guardian's permission. Many online communities require you to be at least thirteen years old or have parental consent to participate.

platform In social media, a platform refers to the social media software for a particular site. Facebook is one platform, Twitter is another, and so on.

social media A collective term for the websites or apps that let users participate in social networking.

social network A dedicated app or website that connects users and allows them to communicate through text posts, messages, images, and so on.

Timeline A Facebook feature that shows your photos and posts, as well as whatever information about yourself that you choose to make public. The Timeline is also sometimes referred to as your profile.

FIND OUT MORE

Books:

Crager, Jamie, Scott Ayres, Melanie Nelson, and Daniel Herndon. *Facebook All-in-One for Dummies.* Hoboken, NJ: Wiley, 2014.

Lamont, Ian. *Twitter in 30 Minutes: How to Connect with Interesting People, Write Great Tweets, and Find Information That's Relevant to You.* Boston: i30 Media Corporation, 2013.

Websites:

Facebook's Tips & Tricks Community Page

www.facebook.com/fbtips

This popular Facebook community page is a place where people can share the latest Facebook tips.

How to Use Twitter Webpage

computer.howstuffworks.com/internet/tips/how-to-use-twitter.htm

This How Stuff Works webpage covers the basics of how to use Twitter and provides a useful list of Twitter-specific terms.

Safer Computing and Social Networks Website

www.usa.gov/topics/science/communications/internet/social-networks.shtml

This useful U.S. government site tells you how to protect yourself on the Internet and on social networks.

BIBLIOGRAPHY

Barnes, Bronwyn. "Bethany Mota: YouTube's Teen Queen." *People*. May 5, 2014.

Curtis, Anthony. "The Brief History of Social Media." University of North Carolina at Pembroke, 2013. http://www2.uncp.edu/home/acurtis/NewMedia/SocialMedia/SocialMediaHistory.html.

"Facebook Statistics." *StatisticBrain.com*, January 1, 2014. http://www.statisticbrain.com/facebook-statistics/.

Federal Trade Commission Bureau of Consumer Protection Business Center. "Children's Online Privacy Protection Rule ('COPPA')." *FTC.gov*. http://www.ftc.gov/enforcement/rules/rulemaking-regulatory-reform-proceedings/childrens-online-privacy-protection-rule.

Fox, Zoe. "How Many Teens Are Actually Leaving Facebook?" *Mashable*, January 16, 2014. http://mashable.com/2014/01/16/teens-leaving-facebook/.

Gobel, Gordon. "The History of Social Networking." *Digital Trends*, September 6, 2012. http://www.digitaltrends.com/features/the-history-of-social-networking/#!NORhj.

Leiner, Barry M., et al. "Brief History of the Internet." *Internet Society*. http://www.internetsociety.org/internet/what-internet/history-internet/brief-history-internet.

Petronzio, Matt. "Everything You Wanted to Know About Facebook Groups." *Mashable*, January 28, 2013. http://mashable.com/2013/01/28/facebook-groups-101/.

Pew Research Center. "Teens Fact Sheet." Pew Research Internet Project. http://www.pewinternet.org/fact-sheets/teens-fact-sheet/.

Phillips, Sarah. "A Brief History of Facebook." *The Guardian*,
July 24, 2007. http://www.theguardian.com/technology/2007/jul/25/media.newmedia.

Reubens, Lindsay. "'Vine-Famous,' This 15-Year-Old Has 1.4 Million Followers Online." *Charlotte Observer*, October 13, 2013. http://www.charlotteobserver.com/2013/10/11/4381277/vine-famous-nash-grier.html#.U3p5GV4mTaU.

Singer, Natasha. "They Loved Your G.P.A. Then They Saw Your Tweets." *New York Times*, November 9, 2013. http://www.nytimes.com/2013/11/10/business/they-loved-your-gpa-then-they-saw-your-tweets.html?_r=0.

INDEX

ABOUT THE AUTHOR

Cathleen Small is an editor, teacher, and author who lives in the greater San Francisco Bay Area. She is an active user of social media, including Facebook, Instagram, and Twitter. She has written several books for Cavendish Square, including two other titles in the Web Wisdom series, *Make the Most of Tumblr and Other Blogging Platforms* and *How to Start an Online Business*. When she's not writing or editing, Cathleen enjoys spending time with her husband, her two young sons (her six-year-old is convinced that he already needs a Facebook account), and her two pugs (who should have their own Facebook account, but are too busy having fun to maintain one!).